TORN
and
TRUE

Bhavya Dixit

Dedicated to: Maa

Thank you, for giving me strength to keep going.

This book is a voice that rises from the depths of
what remains— imperfect, yet whole in the
fragments I've become.

Dear Reader,

I hope these pages offer you the warmth of
understanding, a gentle reminder that you are seen
and heard. You are not alone. Your journey is valid,
and your heart, though it may ache, is whole. Let
this book be the comfort you need, a quiet
affirmation that healing is possible and you
are worthy of it.

I am torn,

But my heart beats true

Healing —

a gentle word,

so pretty it hums like light in the quiet.

It whispers hope

into the hollow spaces,

reminding hearts they're still beating

for a reason.

It tells you:

don't give up.

There's a sunrise waiting

just beyond the night.

Isn't it serene to witness the quiet strength of a person enduring the slow collapse of their world? When everything seems to be going wrong, their heart feels unbearably heavy, the simplest daily tasks become struggles and even sleep becomes a stranger. Yet, in the midst of that storm, that person still wakes up every morning, holding on to the fragile hope that maybe—just maybe, things will get better.

Every day, they gather the shattered pieces of themselves, telling their heart that one day, all of this will make sense. And how surreal, how utterly beautiful, is the courage it takes to keep believing that God has better plans, even when nothing feels right.

After all it's true what they say: Everything goes wrong before everything goes right.

I wear this mask, pretending I'm strong,
But deep down, it feels like everything's wrong.
Adjusting to a life that's now so strange,
A heart broken so deeply, there's no way to change.

I stand in this queue, waiting for a chance,
To move on, to forget, to finally dance.
But the truth is, it's harder than I ever knew,
Each day it hurts more, and I'm feeling so blue.

The children who grew up in a house of pain,
Where fights and abuse echoed again and again,
When they finally leave, they don't see it as defeat
But as an achievement, a victory so sweet.

Leaving behind the tears and sleepless nights
They step into a world where they can rebuild life.
They create a home, not just of walls and a roof,
But a place where peace is real, and their
rights are the truth.

Home—an ache, a question, a comfort I've never held for long.

Now I've found the truth so clear,
No longer ruled by doubt or fear.
Some people leave for our own good,
They knew we loved more than they could.

They break us down with crafted lies,
With poison hidden in disguise.
Not cause we're weak, but strong in grace,
Too bright for them to face our face.

The times we lose the thread of belief,
Slowly carved by the weight of grief.
Waiting for the universe to send a sign,
Till then pretending everything is fine.

The end of the thread still rests in your hand,
Or perhaps it's a truth you fail to understand.
Trying not to surrender faith in the process,
Praying one day you'll be the next one blessed.

Abandonment- such a heavy feeling that sparks a
conflict of emotions: acceptance and self doubt
Everyday you are plucking a rose petal alternatively
asking universe that was it your fault or were they
the traitor.
and no matter what the universe or the people
around you say, you blame yourself thinking you
could have done more and then maybe the situation
would not have been the same.
But abandonment is more than two people parting
ways, the person abandoned learns yearning,
patience, hope and a hard lesson that sometimes
thing are in our own head and the other person is
simply a traitor wrapped in the love we felt for
them.

Isn't it incredible how tiny words—a simple thread of letters and emotions expressed in sentences, sometimes with just a gesture—can break a human heart into countless pieces? Words are among the strongest weapons we have. They come with no remedies to heal and no disclaimers to warn. In just a second, they can shatter someone's heart, crush their hope, and destroy the trust that took years to build. These small, ordinary words are powerful— they reflect who we are and how we choose to treat others.

That's why we must choose our words wisely . Words, once spoken, can change the nature of our relationships, alter the course of someone's life, and turn their world completely upside down. Words should be wrapped in empathy, guided by wisdom, and delivered with care and love. Because I've seen it—how love can turn into stubborn hate, all because of a few painful words. And no matter what you do, you can never fully heal the kind of hurt that words can leave behind.

In this world of manipulation, you truly own this
art
Leaving my scars unseen and tearing my heart
apart
They way you twisted your words masked in the
web of lies
You actually played like a puppet with cruel hidden
ties
And in the midst of those manipulative
confrontations
I relish this new liberating separation.

His gaze has now turned into a cold stare,
Satisfying his whims, so unfair.
Never thought he'd say such harsh things to me,
The scars of disrespect are hard to believe.

He threw his cruel disrespect in my face,
With a sorry, he rests his case.
Is this truly love, or some illusion I'm concealing?
Never thought our bond would end in
silent, aching feeling..

Nowadays, it is so easy to pretend Aesthetic stories showcasing the friendship, family photos concealing the everyday fights,gifts to a partner hiding the absence of love in a relationship. Everything is judged by how perfectly it can be presented to social media.

There were times when real conversations took place in families and among friends but now we have become so busy curating memories that we have forgotten how to live them.

This leave me with an unsettling emptiness as if bonds are losing their spark. Perhaps that is why it is so important that we stop losing ourselves and our capacity to love others just to fit into the picture.

Saying "no" can feel so tough,

But it's the line that keeps you enough.

To guard your peace, your worth, your mind—

Sometimes saying "no" is the kindest sign.

Here's a reminder:

Choose your words carefully, make judgments with empathy and offer criticism with kindness.
Remember, we shape the world with the choices we make and it starts with how we
treat each other.

Somewhere along the way, we lost our sense of empathy and I genuinely cannot stand it.

People have become selfish, indifferent, and strategic in this relentlessly fast-paced world. Instead of trying to understand someone's perspective or asking where they're coming from, we are quick to label them as wrong and move on. But aren't we human?

To be human is to be kind, understanding, and compassionate—not the opposite.

Empathy doesn't make you weak, nor does it make you look uncool. It is one of the rarest strengths a person can possess. Practice empathy not to prove your own goodness, but because every person is fighting a battle you cannot see. Understand others to understand them not to judge or diminish them.

There's something so peaceful about living without rush, without pressure, with nothing to prove or lose, just a little time to laugh, to smile, and to simply be your true self.

When we lose someone who meant the world to us, it's often not the big things we miss — it's the little ones. The hugs, the laughs, the small compliments we never gave, the 'thank yous' we left unspoken.

So today, take a moment. Hug the ones near you. Send a virtual hug to those far away. Say those three magical words: "I love you." Make it a moment that becomes a memory , a small act of love that lasts forever.

Sometimes, the bravest thing we can do is walk away from the people who keep hurting us. Those whose apologies come without change. The ones who only make an effort when you're on the edge of walking away, by then you've already accepted that they'll never love or treat you the way you deserve. And that's okay.Walk away. Take a step back for your own peace, and give yourself the time and space to heal, to love again, and to protect your heart.

 Stop exhausting yourself trying to explain or complain to people who are fully aware of how their careless actions, words, and lies hurt you. The truth is, they know, they just take you for granted. Let those people go. Let that bond go. Accept that it wasn't worthy of your love, and that you deserve far better.

 When holding on feels heavier than letting go, choose yourself. You don't have to carry the weight of someone else's indifference. Let go, and begin your healing for a future that holds peace, love, and everything you truly deserve.

They spoke of love, but in reality, they were the ones who filled me with self-doubt.

The silent walls scream for a new start,
Holding onto the abuse, tearing my heart apart.
Domestic abuse is terrifying, yet it feels habitual,
Living in fear of losing her, a fear perpetual.

I've pushed my desires all aside,
This indifferent, abusive pattern, I've finally
survived.
All of this to bear gives my heart an ache,
I wish they knew the smile I wear is fake.

Alone in corners, my thoughts run wild,
Will someone forgive me, not revile?
Someone who won't shout at my fall,
But gently say, "It's okay, that's all."

Someone to wipe my tear-stained face,
Hold my hand in my darkest place.
To calm my rage, not run away,
But sit beside me and choose to stay.

Too much to write, too much to say,
Too many tears left in the way.
If time permits, I'll sit once more,
Hold their hand and settle the score.

But oh—I forgot, they took that right,
Left me alone in the middle of night.
Now their eyes don't make me feel the same,
They strike with guilt, not love, or flame.

A glance from him so hard to bear,
Could tempt, confuse, or even scare.
That's what our bond had turned into,
A house of storms we never knew.

For a long time, I misunderstood adulting as just doing more—more chores, more studying, more daily tasks piling up. But now, at 18, even though I'm still growing, I've started to realize that adulting isn't just about doing everything on your own. It's about carrying the weight of responsibility with care.

It's learning to care more deeply for the people around you, to step up not just in action, but in presence. Slowly, as you grow, your parents begin to trust you more they take you seriously, and they allow you to make choices for your own good.

Adulting, I've come to learn, isn't about isolating yourself under pressure. It's about growing together, learning to take your family with you and becoming someone who supports and leads with love.

Do you see how productivity has quietly become our identity?

It shapes our mood, our emotions, and even the way we measure our worth. One day of rest makes us feel guilty, as though we've fallen behind everyone else. Students constantly chase the next mock test, the next chapter, the next achievement, believing that doing more automatically means becoming more.

Somewhere along the way, we forgot that productivity isn't measured only by the hours we spend working. An evening spent laughing with your family, a conversation with a friend, a walk with no destination, or simply allowing yourself to breathe without guilt—those moments are productive too. They restore the very person who is expected to keep going.

Working hard is important, but when productivity becomes your personality, rest begins to feel like failure. And that is where we lose ourselves.

Sometimes the most productive thing you can do is to simply exist without trying to earn your worth.

Have you ever paused, just for a while,
To watch how life moves on, mile by mile?
It doesn't stop for hearts that ache,
Or for the bonds we thought would never break.

We laugh again, we learn to smile,
Without the ones who stayed a while.
The ones we swore we couldn't outlive,
Yet here we are, with more to give.

Growth is a quiet miracle.

It reminds us that growing up doesn't just mean getting older—it means gaining maturity, courage, strength, and above all, acceptance.

When someone throws disrespect in your face, places blame on you, or questions your character, don't waste your time explaining or justifying yourself. Instead, gather the courage to walk away. The people who truly love you will never question your worth—they'll never burden you with blame or cause you pain. Those who genuinely care for you will uplift you, not tear you down.

And in the middle of it all,

I find myself thinking—

About the invisible weight each one carries,

The battles we fight in silence,

The responsibilities that press against our shoulders,

Sometimes too heavy to hold.

We blame ourselves, we search for flaws,
Wondering what had bent the laws.
Was it our fault they walked away?
Did we not love them the right way?

Forget the moments that made you cry,"
The heavy hearts and last goodbye,
Don't fear the storm or shifting flow—
For people change as they come and go.

At dawn, the loud voices rise again,
I flinch and freeze, bracing the pain.
At times I wish to run, to just disappear,
But then I see her eyes, heavy with tears.

Yes, I might fly far, away from this fight,
But she'll remain trapped in that cold, endless
night.
No hand to hold her, no voice to soothe,
No one to tell her she'll pull through.

And then creeps in that darkest fear—
What if she breaks... and I'm not near?
How would I survive, how would I go on,
If one day I woke up and she was gone?

I wish,to no longer pray just for peace and calm,
instead to built a home that is safe and warm.

To feel the wind of freedom in your soul,
To know there are no chains, no walls to hold,
Where you stand as the master of your fate,
Living life as you chose, no need to wait.

No contradictions in the choices you make,
No guilt in the paths that you decide to take.
You are the truth that the world will see,
In liberty, you live and simply be.

I know they'll judge me for my marks,
For shattered dreams and hidden scars.
They'll judge the choices I regret,
The steps I took, the tears I've wept.

They'll call me lost, say I'm to blame,
For not becoming someone great.
For every "no" I couldn't fight,"
And every flaw I failed to hide.

But what they miss behind my eyes,
Is not a plea to sympathize.
Why can't they understand, I try each day
To hold myself in my own way.

I am a thread woven of hope, strength, and tears.

I wish it were easier to voice the pain and discomfort women experience every single day. I wish women didn't have to constantly prove that they have a right to live freely, boldly, and on their own terms. I wish there wasn't a patriarchal manual quietly passed down—telling women how to be a good daughter, a good sister, a good wife, or a good mother.

Isn't it ironic how the very people who fail to be good humans are the ones so eager to define what a woman should be in every role? Let women live as humans first, and you'll witness the magic they bring into the world.

There's such a heartbreaking dichotomy in our country—where women are celebrated during the day, and molested under the cover of night. How deeply I wish to celebrate womanhood, to embrace its power and beauty. But how can I, when justice is delayed, patriarchy is normalized, and voices of orthodox men still dominate the narrative?

Women should be given what they truly deserve—not questioned endlessly about whether the liberties granted to them are "enough." Men may never fully understand the silent pain women endure every single day—especially at night, when fear becomes a constant companion. It's tragic that we must call a victim someone's daughter or sister just to gain sympathy, as if being a woman alone isn't reason enough to care.

I hope we build a world where women don't have to survive with fear, but can finally live with freedom. A world where being a woman is not a risk, but a reason to rise.

Will someone love me, raw and true—

The way I feel, the way I do?

Will someone fear to lose me, too,

As I do for the precious few?

My illusion shattered, hope turned dim,

And I fell into shadows, cold and grim.

They broke the trust I gave so pure,

They loved, then lied, and closed the door.

He left me alone with a thousand doubts,
I close my eyes and still hear his shouts.
The love has withered—it's painfully clear,
Leaving behind nothing but silence and fear.

His insecurities became my chains,
I searched for answers but found only pain.
I wished he'd return to the man that I knew,
Instead, I became the one he broke into.

Silence took over me slowly with a heart burdened
by truths that were left unheard.

Understand this—

You deserve to stand in the light

of those who see your value

without needing it spelled out,

without conditions,

without hesitation.

Do not let careless words

or loveless actions

dim the truth of who you are.

Hope is what gives us the courage to keep moving when nothing seems to be changing. It is the quiet belief that our hard work will one day bear fruit, that every unanswered prayer has not gone unheard, and that even when life feels uncertain, God is still writing a story we cannot yet understand.

Faith reminds us that life is more than struggle, disappointment, and tears. It asks us to trust that joy exists beyond today's hardships, that love will find its way to us, and that every season of pain carries the possibility of growth.

Perhaps hope doesn't promise that tomorrow will be easier, it simply whisper that tomorrow is worth reaching.

Have you noticed how easy it has become to judge others these days? Life seems to be moving faster than ever, with trends changing every two days, and people—along with their words—becoming the next meme. It's become effortless to judge or troll someone based on the smallest things, like the aesthetic of their bio, the style of their profile picture, or the stories they post.

But have you ever stopped to think about the public figures behind the content? In the name of criticism, we've crossed a line— rape threats, acid attack threats, and hate-filled comments have become tragically common in our society. We've become so caught up in our own lives that we've stopped considering the impact of our words on others.

People see so many different shades of us. Some see the joyful version—the one who smiles endlessly, full of life. But behind that façade are the real ones—the ones who have seen us shattered, broken, and quietly falling apart. They've witnessed the struggles, they've seen us hide our pain, our scars, even the moments we tried to give up.

Then there are those who see the inspiring version of us—wrapped in confidence, chasing dreams we once only whispered about. And there are those who've seen us in our darkest phases, picking up the shattered pieces of our hearts after unexpected failures. Some call us clever, bold, even full of attitude. Some say we're beautiful, inside and out.

But through it all, we come to realize: some people will only ever see the surface—but the real ones, they look deeper. They hold our hand through the storms, they stay, they endure. They feel the weight of our pain without ever needing to be asked.

Each day begins with the same old fight,

While I calm my panic out of sight.

I soothe myself, whisper, "You'll survive,"

And brace for whatever may arrive.

I know so many people in life are fake,

They break you down, then walk away.

With empty words, they soothe, they lie—

And leave us alone with no goodbye.

Anger doesn't warn with words—it strikes
with wounds.

When I'm left in silence and space,I fall apart,
pieces all over the place.

Emotions are whole , raw and breathtakingly pure.
They are never excessive ,never counterfeit. They
complete our lives, our bonds and the fragile spaces
within us and when you find someone before whom
you can bare your truest and most veritable self, life
feels a little lighter, a little more complete

Peace doesn't always come from solving
everything— sometimes, it's found in letting go, in
small pauses, in moonlit windows
and midnight roads.

This is a reminder: be your true self.

Be beautiful.

Be brave.

Be bold.

Be benevolent.

Be blessed.

Kindness isn't owed, but given,
To hearts that know the art of living—
With gentle hands and honest grace,
Not empty words or a hollow face.

So when you find the warmth withdrawn,
Ask what you gave before it's gone.
The rule is simple, clear, and known:
You only reap what you have sown.

Gratitude is a beautiful feeling — a quiet realization
of how lucky we are to be surrounded by people
who love us just as we are. People who admire our
simplest quirks, who support us through every
storm, and who stand by us like the strongest
pillars — friends, siblings, family, well-wishers.

Gratitude makes life feel more surreal, more loving,
and beautifully simple. It gives us the comfort of
knowing that we're not alone — that we have a
shoulder to lean on when the world feels heavy.

Beauty —in the quiet strength of those who hold it all together, even as their world quietly burns.

Sometimes, we all go through phases in life where everything feels wrong. Our hearts feel heavy, and our spirits seem incapable of expressing what's really going on inside. We avoid the simple question — 'Are you okay?' — because we don't even know how to answer it.

Every day feels suffocating and mentally draining, where all we want to do is sleep or cry our hearts out. Our minds become crowded with self-doubt, fears of failure, and insecurities. In times like these, it can feel like life has defeated us — like everything is over.

But trust me when I say this: after the storm comes the calm. The phase that feels like the end of everything will pass. And you will feel better. You will feel lighter, happier, and eventually, everything will come together — and it'll all be worth it.

Not every "rejection" is loss or lack—

Some closed-off roads don't lead us back.

Some dreams we hold are not our own,

Just stepping stones to the unknown.

One day you will find yourself reminiscing and
you'll wonder-
If I still live on cups of cold coffee,
If I still tear up at th movies I've seen a hundred
times,
If I still let my typos slip by without care,
If I still crave ice cream even with a sore throat,
If I still retreat into silence when my heart aches,
and If I still look to the universe for signs trying to
bind destiny and everyone together.

I wore their lies like gloves upon my heart but
instead of warmth, they brought only doubt and
fear.
Cold as frost, they turned me blue not shileding me
from betrayal, but crushing my heart into
splintered pieces.
Those fragments pierced my bones,hollowing me
out from within.
Instead of strength I was left numb learning how to
be.

"Memories are a juxtaposition of a gentle embrace and the sting of absence"

What you lost was life's quiet art, to mend your soul, not break your heart.

How beautiful it is—

to laugh carelessly, wildly,

with that one friend

who feels more like family.

The one who's seen

every shade of your soul—

the bright, the broken,

the silent, the storm.

And still, they stand.

Firmly.

Quietly holding your hand

through it all.

It's friendships like these

that remind me

how truly beautiful

human bonds can be.

Your worth is not up for debate.

It is yours.

Yours to define.

Yours to protect.

Yours to live.

Feeling helpless is the worst emotions of all,
surrounded by so many, yet no one to call.
So you sit down and pray, and sometimes
consumed in rage,
Just want to take your mother and yourself out
from the cage.

It hurts me from within to experience this every
day, every night.
Will I ever experience a home where the sun shines
bright,
Instead of this place where I live,
Where the walls contain our dreadful
and silent cries?

There is a void inside me that people are creating,
The memories of happier days are slowly fading.
Seeing him abuse, I feel lost and estranged,
Anxiety doesn't scare me, but I am scared of his
rage.

How will I ever overcome this childhood fear?
The frightening sights are impossible to bear.
I thought I was living with the people I love the
most,
But this family feels like a haunted
house without ghosts.

Have you ever felt that strange, empty silence after a panic attack? You just sit there—quiet, still—after crying your heart out, and all you feel is... nothing. A deep emptiness. A loneliness so heavy it aches.

 You start to believe that maybe it's over—that your heart can't take one more failure, one more loss. You're drowning in doubt, in fear of what's coming next. Anxiety wraps around you like a storm, and your dreams feel shattered into pieces too small to fix. On days like that, it feels like everything has ended.

But one day—when you've grown stronger, when you've healed, when you're standing tall with a brave heart and a steady mind—you'll look back. And you'll realize: those painful moments didn't break you. They built you. They shaped your strength and made you into the powerful, resilient person you are today.

Leaving behind what hurts isn't giving up - it's choosing yourself.

Her anger, her moods, they easily show,
But not the sorrow buried below.
They say she's naive, can't read her mind—
But deep inside, she's just confined.

She acts like nothing gets to her,
But inside, emotions start to stir.
She fears too much, she tries to trust,
Yet slips again, as she knows she must.

She claims she's enough, doesn't need a hand,
But longs for someone to understand.
To offer a shoulder, hear her through,
Not fix her, just stay true.

So she keeps meeting people, seeking light,
Still ends up alone in the quiet night.
Among them all, she plays her part,
Yet silence lingers in her heart.

“Familiar hearts wear unfamiliar faces now.”

I read about spiral dynamics once, a map of how people and societies grow in the way they think and see the world. In the yellow stage, life is no longer black and white, it reveals itself as a vast and interconnected.

This made me realize a harsh truth, people dont always change their opinion, sometimes they simply enter Yellow, where blame dissovw and perspective expands. Perhaps this is what we should learn too: not too crumble in agony, but to accept and to find a gentler way of walking through the complexity of a malevolent world.

One day,

you will smile again—

not because the pain vanished,

but because you learned to live beside it.

The broken pieces?

They'll come together,

not as they once were,

but as something stronger—

a reflection of everything

you were meant to become.

"True grace lies in how we love ourselves—healing,
growing, and giving the love we freely offer others."

"In the quiet embrace of freedom, you discover the true essence of your soul."

Will I ever find love that feels like home?
A space to belong, where I'm not alone?
Each night I wipe my tears away,
Curl into silence and drift away

From those we should receive love and grace,
Why must we endure pain in that very place?
Seeing other families laugh and live whole,
Plants a quiet longing deep in my soul.

"Do not bend your soul to fit into the mould of
someone else's shallow love."

"The quiet voice of courage within you carries the greatest power."

"You are the sum of every tear, every smile, every misstep, and every victory."

I used to panic whenever I couldn't figure things out. There was a certain satisfaction in having everything under control—following a to-do list, tackling backlogs, and knowing exactly what needed to be done.

 I liked the structure, the certainty, and the feeling of having a grip on life. Sudden changes or unexpected situations where I felt lost made me uncomfortable. I didn't like feeling blank or unsure of what to do next.

But now, I feel differently. I've come to realize through some tough experiences that life's unpredictability isn't something to fear. Sudden changes, ups and downs, and even moments of confusion often come with valuable lessons and unexpected motivation.

I've learned that it's not always necessary to have everything figured out or to always be in control. Sometimes, it's okay to let things flow, to trust the process, and to let the universe set the pace. Our job is to stay mindful, do our best, and not let uncertainty steal our peace. It's okay to not know, to feel lost sometimes, and to not have all the answers right away.

I once believed, betrayal was simply not being chosen, but it is simply far crueler. When they do choose you, but only to wound, to drown your heart in despair, to leave you drowning in blue.

Shift your gaze, and you may see,
Not all that's lost was meant to be.
The doors once begged to let you through
Were never built with you in view.

The universe, both vast and wise,
May hide its gifts in strange disguise.
It pulls you back—not out of spite,
But to redirect your flight.

They say hurt makes you strong, but how can
something that shatters you into pieces ever make
you stronger?
The truth is, it leaves you feeling blue. Too drained
to even shed a tear, Too numb to grieve, Too broken
to voice your agony.

In this endless tug-of-war between strength and
weakness, we often forget to truly feel the weight of
pain, to allow ourselves the grace of simply being
not okay.

That is what hurt does, it leaves you too fragile to
trust again. Too weary to restart, Too weak to
believe in healing.

For many years of my life, I thought I was a city girl, someone who loved busy streets, twinkling lights, and the hum of constant movement. I believed I was the kind of person who thrived in chaotic gatherings, dancing freely at loud parties, surrounded by large, friendly groups, talking about the latest trends and laughing without a care in the world.

But somewhere along the way, things shifted. Now, I find myself craving something softer. I love quiet, comforting places, wrapped in nature where I'm sitting with the people I love most, sipping a warm mug of coffee, sharing our favorite meals.

The conversations are slower now. They're not about trends, but about growth, peace, dreams, and the struggles we quietly carry.

This change in my preferences has taught me something simple yet profound: change is constant. And maybe that's the beauty of life — learning to embrace who you are in each new chapter.

I've hidden the memories where I can't see,

Locked in a place that's not for me.

But sometimes I pause and let them flow,

And remember the love I had to outgrow.

I never noticed how time slipped by,
Trying to hold them close, help them try.
Yet the fake ones used my pain for gain,
Left me more shattered, deep in strain.

They walked away instead of being my light
And broke the trust I held so tight.
Still, I've learned and I carry that weight,
With every scar, I recreate.

Isn't it strange — even heartbreaking — how people who were once such a huge part of our lives can, one random day, tear our hearts into pieces and walk away like we meant nothing? Just like that.

They leave us in the middle of our misery, shaken, scared, and unsure if we'll ever feel safe in someone again. Do people even realize how their smallest actions, their careless jokes, can leave behind wounds that don't just fade — wounds that turn into lifelong insecurities?

What's even harder is watching the very people who promised to protect us become the reason we're hurting. The ones we trusted the most become the source of our self-doubt, fear, and emotional scars — scars that may never fully heal.

But to those people, I have just one thing to say: karma exists. God is watching. Please, think before you hurt someone. Don't make light of someone's feelings. Don't turn love or trust into a weapon. Be better. Choose kindness. And maybe, just maybe, start seeing life and people through a lens of empathy.

The desire to seek love again has now finished

Whenever I see myself in the mirror,

I feel lost and incomplete.

The wounds expose my insecurity and anxiety,

A pinch of smile shows my strength,

The mirror reveals my vulnerability,

And my acceptance defines who I am.

"Changing isn't a loss; it's the art of awakening."

I was a girl with so many dreams,

But now I'm only left with silent screams.

In my defence, I want to say I tried,

But still, no one's ever satisfied.

I want to scream, I want to shout out loud,

I want to say things, to say them proud

No one's with me, I repeat, none,

And I'm lost in this battle I can't have won.

As my final act of love,
I will leave this house, this place that never felt like
home, never felt like love. Where I woke up with
swollen eyes, with guilt and helplessness and a
simple question
What did I do to deserve being here?

Anger wraps around my bones,
helplessness grows into regret,
and together they whisper,
You cannot live here anymore

Not here,
Not anywhere,
Because somewhere along the way,
I stopped living
and only learned to look alive.

She shines in crowd but fades when alone—hurt by
the ones she once called home.

Live each moment, bold and true,

Embrace the now in all you do.

Let no regret be left behind,

For hope is the light we find.

Do not burden your heart

with the weight of darker days,

they are only shadows

meant to fade.

Our bond lingers like the sweet scent of a broken crayon—hopeful, yet shattered.

Sometimes, the truth may shatter a soul, but it is the only way to clear the fog and make everything crystal clear. Telling lies just to hold things together or to mask reality is never the right path. Even if your truth may cause pain, do not be afraid to speak it. Do not cover it with the honey of lies, let truth stand, pure and unmasked.

Thank You

Thank you for staying. For spending time with these pages. If even a single line met you where you needed it, or held your heart a little softer, then this was worth writing. May you carry its comfort with you, and the gentle reminder that even when you're torn your essence stays true.

it ends here